How to Draw
PETS

Barbara Soloff Levy

Dover Publications, Inc.
Mineola, New York

Note

Pets are lots of fun, and so is learning how to draw pictures of them! In this entertaining and challenging book, you will learn to create pictures of a variety of pets, using just a few simple shapes and lines. Every page, except pages 4, 8, and 52, has four steps to follow to draw one pet (page 4 has two different puppies, page 8 has two different kittens, and page 52 has three types of tropical fish).

For step one, draw the basic shape, using a pencil in case you want to make any changes later on. For steps two, three, and four, you will add details to your picture. Some of the pictures have dotted lines—you can erase these lines as a final step. When you are happy with your drawing, go over the lines with a felt-tip pen or colored pencil. Of course, you can keep working on your drawing, too, erasing and then drawing in new lines until you are pleased with the results. Finally, feel free to color your drawing any way you wish!

After you finish this book, you can use your new skills and your imagination to draw pictures of other pets and animals. Have fun!

Bibliographical Note

How to Draw Pets is a new work, first published by
Dover Publications, Inc., in 2006.

International Standard Book Number

ISBN-13: 978-0-486-44710-0
ISBN-10: 0-486-44710-3

Manufactured in the United States by LSC Communications
44710318   2017
www.doverpublications

How to Draw
PETS

2 Dog

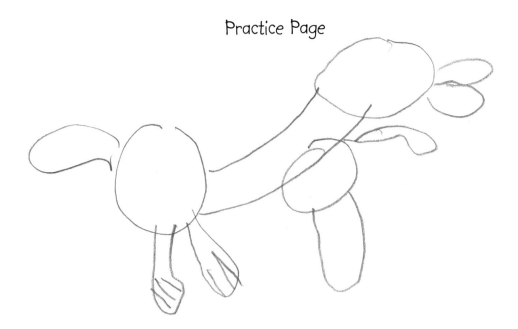

1

2

1

2

12   Gerbil

Practice Page

18 Parrot

20 Canary

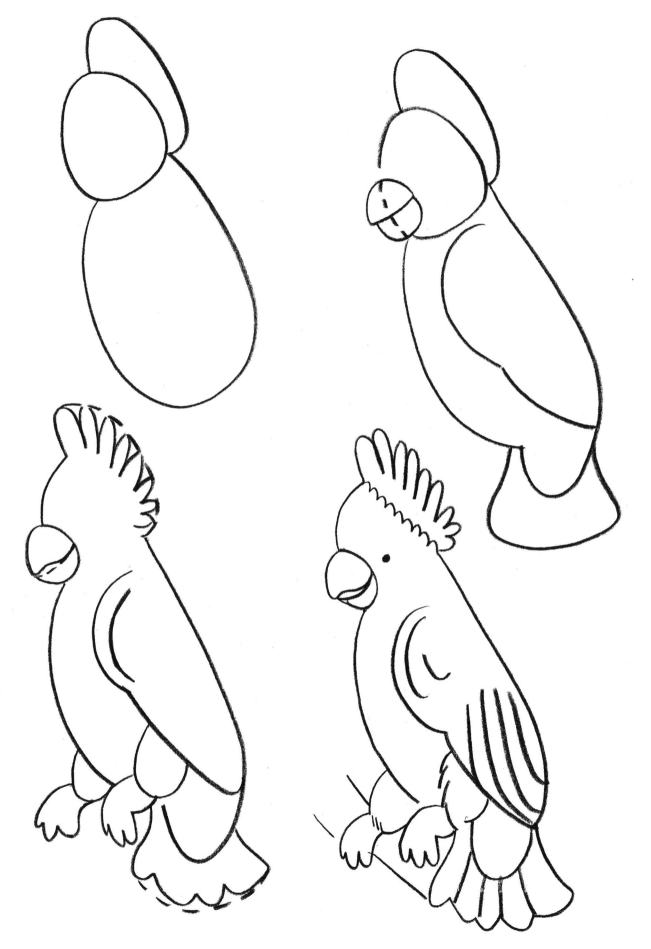

Practice Page

Practice Page

28   Chick

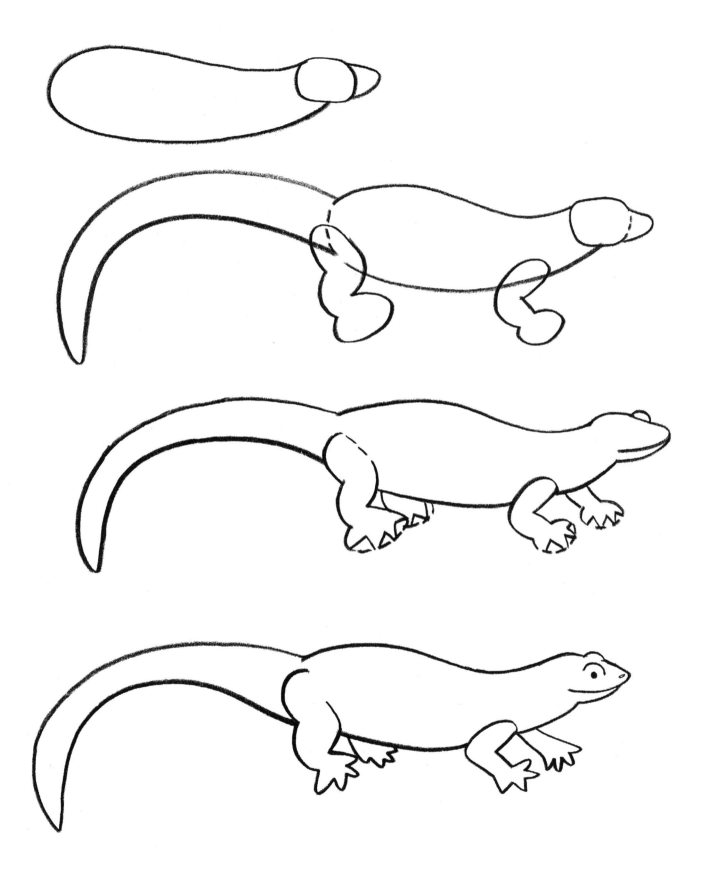

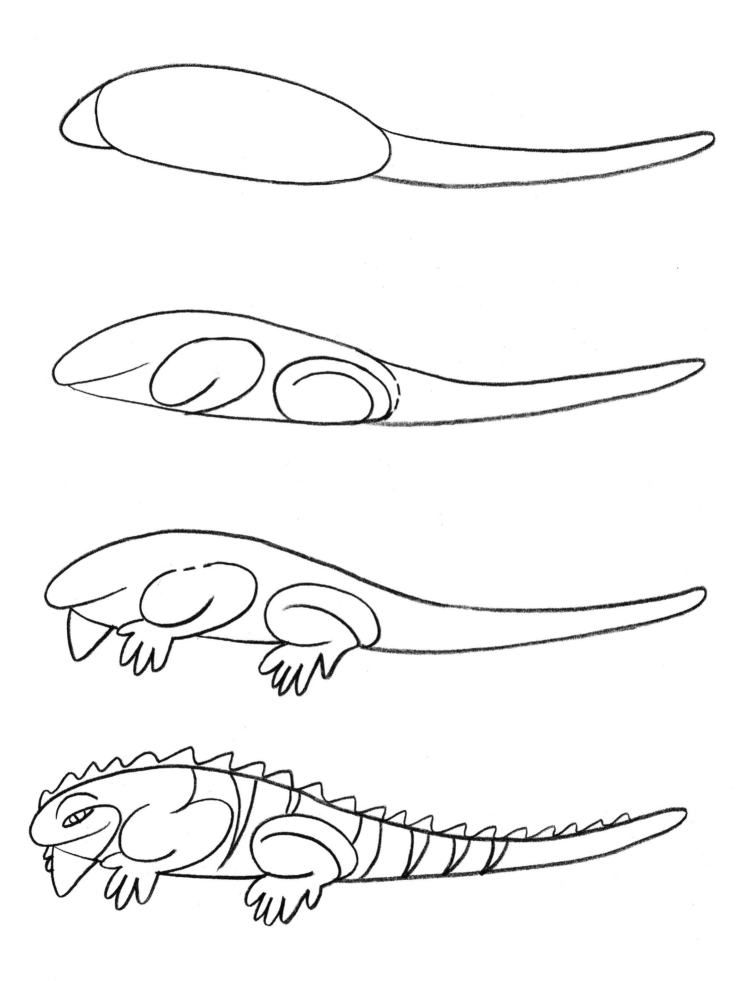

38 Ferret

46   Guinea Pig

Swordtail

Guppy

Angelfish

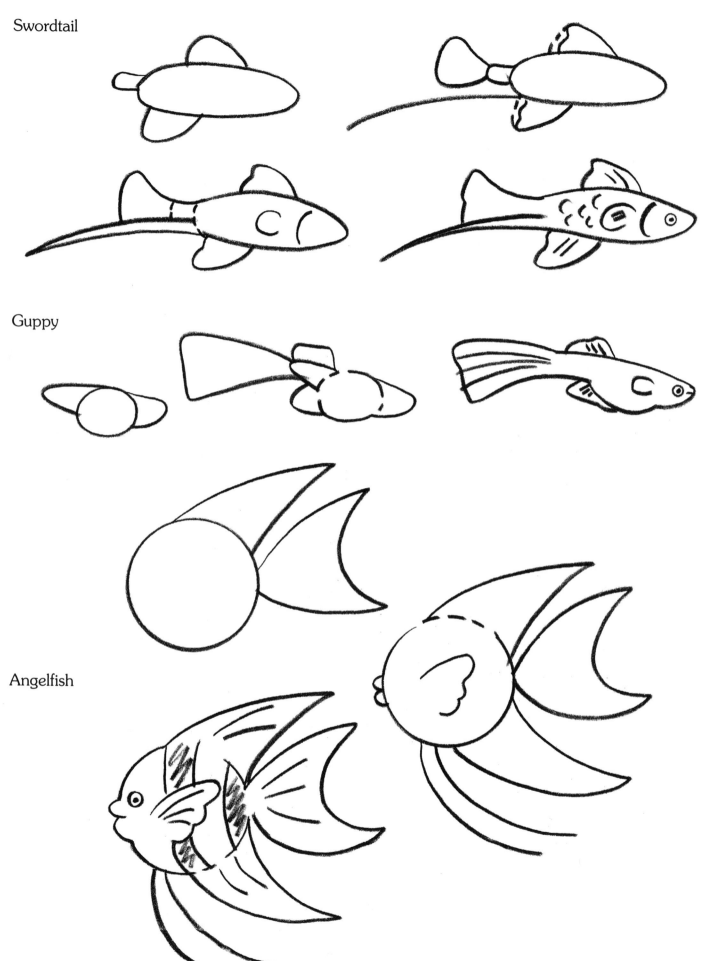

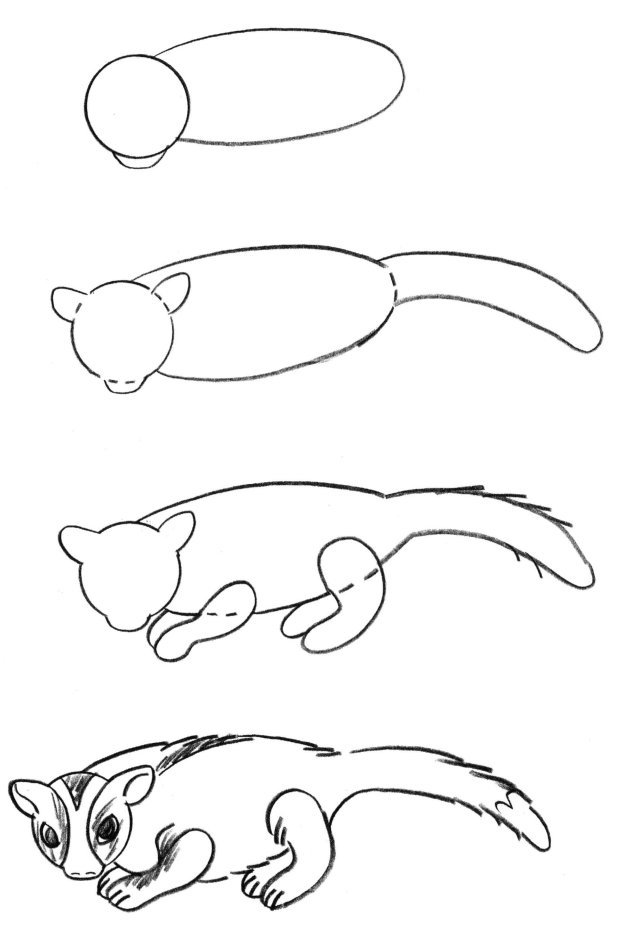

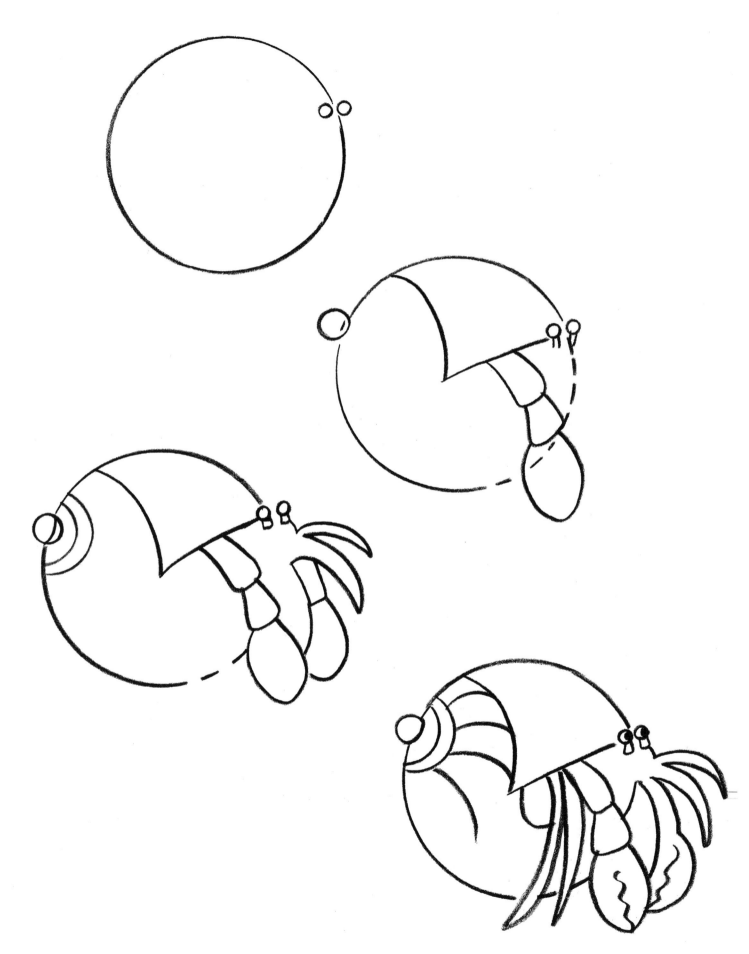

Practice Page